INTRODUCTION

WHAT SORT OF HOUSE do you live in? What is it made of? What does it look like? Did your family build it themselves? How many people live there? Is it warm in winter and cool in summer?

From the beginning of time, people all around the world have used local materials in ingenious ways to provide shelter from the weather, dangerous animals and unfriendly neighbours.

Over many generations, in countless tiny settlements, people have tackled the problems posed by their local conditions to build their own individual styles of housing. Once evolved, these styles remained largely unchanged for centuries.

All the traditional homes in this book are still being used today. But the old skills and time-honoured ways of building are gradually disappearing and being replaced by modern methods. In another generation, many of the houses shown here will, sadly, have gone for ever.

This book is divided into five sections.

Each section covers two or three examples. For each example there is an overall view of the house and its locality, together with plans, elevations, cross-sections and detailed sketches. There is also a written description of the way it was built and why, and a little about the family that lives there, and their community.

Most of these houses date from a time when bath-rooms and toilets did not exist. You can see from the plans that in some cases (particularly mobile homes) they still do not. But in most cases, modern plumbing has been added.

Although many of these houses are hundreds or even thousands of years old, a few, like the *Queenslander* on pages 28 and 29, are more recent and have been included because they are tried and true styles of building, using local materials to suit local conditions, just as the older ones are.

HOMEMADE HOUSES

TRADITIONAL HOMES FROM MANY LANDS

JOHN NICHOLSON

A LITTLE ARK BOOK

ALLEN & UNWIN

Also by John Nicholson,
from Allen & Unwin:

Paper Chase
A Frantic Dash Around The World
by Land, Sea and Air

A Little Ark Book
First published 1993 by
Allen & Unwin Pty Ltd
9 Atchison Street
St Leonards, NSW 2065
Australia
10 9 8 7 6 5 4 3 2

National Library of Australia
Cataloguing-in-Publication entry:

Nicholson, John, 1950- .
   Homemade houses.

   ISBN 1 86373 489 9. (hb)
   ISBN 1 86373 516 X. (pb)

   1.Dwellings – Design and construction –
   Juvenile literature. I. Title.

728.37

Set in Cochin by Pixel Pty Ltd, Melbourne
Printed in Hong Kong by Dah Hua Printing

1
MOBILE HOMES

IN THE WILDEST and most inhospitable regions on earth, people have survived for thousands of years by wandering from place to place in search of pastures for their animals, and food and water for themselves.

The wandering peoples of desert, plains and tundra have collapsible homes which they can transport easily and assemble quickly.

Moroccan Tent

Fatima lives in a tent in the hot, dry desert country of southern Morocco. Her family has a herd of sheep and goats which they move regularly from place to place in search of feed and water. Their tent goes with them.

In the desert there is really only one available building material: cloth made from animal hair or wool. The black tents used by numerous wandering peoples across a huge area, from Morocco in the west to Jordan and Saudi Arabia in the east, are all made of cloth woven from sheeps' wool or goat hair. They all use small amounts of wood for poles, pegs (for

TOP OF TENT POLES

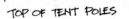

GUY ROPES

attaching guy ropes and walls to the tent) and special sockets designed to stop the tops of the poles from wearing or ripping the tent fabric.

The overall shape of the tents varies from region to region. Fatima's tent has a distinctive hump-back shape held up by a collection of diagonal tent poles.

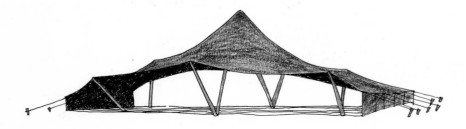

Inside, the tent is divided into two areas: one for the men and one for the women.

During the day, the walls are rolled up to allow cooling breezes to blow through the tent. At night, they are rolled down and sealed at the bottom, while fires are lit inside. For sleeping, mattresses are brought out and laid on the rugs that cover the ground.

Fatima's family cooks on an open fire or in an oven pit, outside the tent.

AFGHAN YURT

Akbar lives high in the remote Pamir Mountains somewhere near the border separating Afghanistan and Tadzhikistan. His tiny village is home to twenty-four people. There is one stone building, several animal enclosures and four *yurts*.

A yurt is a circular tent made of heavy felt or canvas draped over an elaborate framework of willow sticks. Nomadic peoples of central Asia have used yurts for thousands of years as they roam the enormous mountainous area from Iran in the west to Mongolia in the east.

LATTICE WALL PANELS ARE COMPRESSED FOR TRANSPORTATION

The walls are made of expanding sheets of timber lattice, or trellis. Three or four sheets are tied together to form a circular enclosure with a door frame at one point. At the top of the wall, a strong rope is tied right around the yurt to stop the heavy roof pushing the walls out.

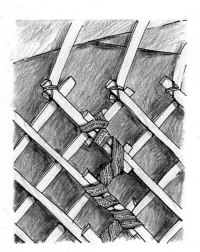

The ends of a large number of willow sticks are slightly bent, then tied to the top of the walls. The other ends of the sticks all meet in the middle and are tied to a small timber ring at the top of the roof. The whole thing is then covered in thick felt, or canvas sheets which are securely tied on.

Two people can put up a yurt in about half an hour.
When packed up, it can be carried by two camels.

Inside, there are felt mats and brightly coloured
cushions on the floor, and an open fire burning yak
dung in the middle of the room. The smoke escapes
through an opening in the roof, but this hole can
be covered up to keep out the cold air.

During the summer months, Akbar's
family moves up to the higher
mountains to find fresh
pastures for their sheep
and yaks. They take
their yurt, and
set up house
wherever it
suits them.

INUIT IGLOO

Aitoak lives in a small fishing village on the coast of northern Alaska. Her people call themselves the Inuit, which means "the People".

Aitoak's family lives for most of the year in a modern timber house in a permanent settlement. But on their regular hunting and fishing trips inland, along the coast, or out onto the sea-ice, they often build the traditional snow domes, known as *igloos*.

Experienced Inuit can build a snow dome in an hour. First they cut blocks of carefully chosen snow and lay them together in an ascending spiral. Each block leans inward slightly until the very top is reached.

CROSS-SECTION

FLOOR PLAN

They seal the joints with loose snow, and then fit the final block. Next, they light a lamp inside the dome and let the heat from the lamp melt the snow on the inside. Then they put out the lamp, and let cold wind blow into the igloo.

This freezes the melted snow, and forms a smooth lining of ice which keeps out any draughts. They cover the icy walls and ceiling with skins and rugs for added insulation, and to prevent the warmth within from melting the dome.

The entry is a snow tunnel which may pass through one or more smaller domes used for storage. The entrance tunnel is usually built with several changes of direction so that the cold wind can't blow straight into the living areas.

Above the entry is a small window made of seal intestines, or a sheet of clear ice, carefully carried with the family from camp site to camp site.

Aitoak sleeps in the main dome on a platform raised above floor level. The floor here is higher than the tunnel floor. Since hot air always rises above cold air, the sleeping platforms remain the warmest part of the igloo.

Often, several families join igloos together and share some rooms. Aitoak's family is sharing the igloo shown here with another family.

On long hunting trips, the Inuit still use their reliable dog sleds, even though they have skidoos and snowmobiles which they use around their home towns.

Here are two more mobile homes still being used today. Very few of
the traditional gypsy caravans pictured above are still in use in
England and Europe, but throughout the world many people still live
in caravans.

Millions of people in Asia live on the water in boats moored in
settlements like this one in Shanghai.

2
HOUSES OF REED, GRASS AND BAMBOO

PLANTS FLOURISH IN the hot, steamy islands and coastal regions of the tropics, providing good supplies of grasses, leaves, bamboo and timber for building.

In these areas, houses are designed to allow the cooling sea breezes to waft through unimpeded by walls. The roofs are large, steep and built in bold shapes, to shed the heavy rain and provide plenty of shade.

The Malay village pictured above is actually built over the water, which is cooler than the land. Villagers can catch fish for dinner just outside their front door.

MADAN MUDHIF

Abdul lives in a *mudhif*.

In southern Iraq, along the lower reaches of the Tigris and Euphrates rivers, live the Madan people, or Marsh Arabs. They inhabit hundreds of small islands scattered over an area of 160,000 square kilometres.

Each island of mud and reeds has its own buffalo paddock, several boats and a mudhif, or house.

To build their house, Abdul and his family gather a large quantity of a local reed which grows as high as

six metres.
The reeds are tied
into bundles, called *fasces*,
stuck into the ground in pairs
about five or six metres apart, bent over
at the top and lashed together to form a series of
arches. Mats woven from split reeds form the walls
and roof.

Inside, is one large room, with no furniture except for
carpets on the floor, and a cooking hearth. Delicately
patterned openings let in light and air.

A mudhif does not last long because the
reeds rot rapidly in the wet conditions. New
reeds grow quickly, however, and are
easily cut and bundled, so these large and
imposing structures can be regularly
rebuilt when necessary.

The Madan people have been
regularly rebuilding mudhifs
for over five thousand years.

SULAWESI TONGKONAN

Andi, Ratha and Hasan live in a *tongkonan*, a traditional upper-class or nobles' house from the Tanatoraja region of Sulawesi, in Indonesia.

Their family's small but very ornate house took many months to build. Each stage of the construction was marked by elaborate ceremonies. When the tongkonan was finally finished, a buffalo, four pigs, and many chickens were sacrificed, and a huge feast was prepared for the whole village.

These special houses, which only the nobility may build and occupy, have been built in the same way for centuries. The floor sits on many thick, round poles about two metres high. The floor and walls are framed in smooth, squared timber. All the framework is slotted together so that no nails are needed. The large roof is shaped like a saddle, with very high gable ends, angled outwards and each supported by its own special pole. The roof frame and the roof covering are made entirely of bamboo.

The gables (ends of the roof) are decorated with painted geometric designs and a carving of a buffalo's head.

Inside, the tongkonan is divided into three rooms: a living room and two bedrooms, with very small doorways. The living room has an open hearth for cooking.

ROOF SPACE SOMETIMES CONTAINS UPPER LEVEL GALLERIES

CROSS-SECTION

Once European building techniques were introduced to the area, fewer of these beautiful houses were built. Today, there is a revival of the old ways. New tongkonans are being built again, and many old ones are being restored.

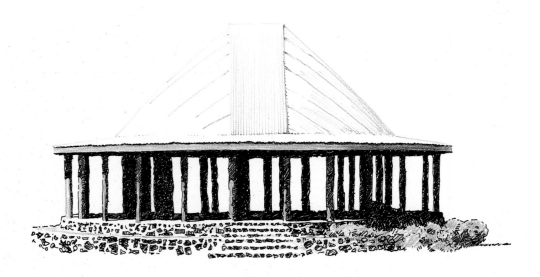

If you walk through a Samoan village you can look right into all the *fales*, or houses. The open sides do have blinds, however, which are lowered at night or when it rains heavily. Look at the way in which a modern material, corrugated iron, has been adapted to the traditional roof shape.

The house below, in Venezuela, looks like an example of how not to build a comfortable house for a hot climate. With only one doorway, and a tiny smoke hole in the roof, it must be stifling inside! In fact the inhabitants move out during the hottest months.

3 HOUSES OF EARTH AND CLAY

MUD, OR CLAY is a useful and versatile building material, second only to timber. These days, we make bricks and tiles out of it. Traditionally, it has been put to use for the floor, walls and roofs of houses, and the furniture, ovens, fireplaces and plumbing fittings. It has been widely used in areas where grasses, timber and stone were not available.

The illustration above is a bird's-eye view of Fez, in Morocco; a jumble of more or less rectangular rooms and houses with flat roofs and tiny courtyards separated here and there by narrow twisting lanes and walkways—all made of mud.

DOGON VILLAGE

Balpa and Sanu live in a village called Sanga, two hundred and forty kilometres from the ancient and fabled city of Timbuktu. Sanga is one of many villages strung out along a 145 kilometre stretch of high cliffs, called Bandiragara, which is home to the Dogon people.

Balpa's and Sanu's house is a series of mud brick rooms; some square or rectangular, some circular, grouped around an open courtyard. The mud brick walls are plastered with more mud and straw. Before the rainy season, starting in June, this protective coating is patched and repaired.

The roofs are flat, built of logs and mud, and sometimes supported by timber posts. Balpa and Sanu climb ladders to sleep up there during the hot, dry months.

The family has two granaries, or storehouses. The one containing large stocks of grains is the responsibility of the father. He keeps it sealed with mud in case the grain is needed in future years when harvests are not so plentiful. The other one, with everyday supplies of grains, vegetables, other food and household items, is the mother's responsibility.

Wealthy families have more than just two granaries (sometimes as many as ten). They

CROSS-SECTION

MOTHER'S STORE

COURTYARD

CHILDREN'S BEDROOM

LIVING ROOM

KITCHEN

FATHER'S STORE

FLOOR PLAN

are kept well stocked with grain, and are a sign of the family's position in the community.

The granaries are built in the same way as the houses, except that some are built up on rough timber supports because the ground is steep and rocky. They also have conical straw roofs built over their flat mud roofs for added protection.

Sanga is built among the boulders and rubble at the base of a 200-metre-high cliff. Its narrow, crooked lanes and irregular-shaped houses and courtyards are arranged among huge fallen boulders, narrow canyons and outcrops of rock.

Above, a few buildings are precariously perched among hollowed out caverns in the cliff. Below, the flat land is reserved for growing vital food crops of millet, sorghum, rice and beans.

CAPPADOCIAN CAVE

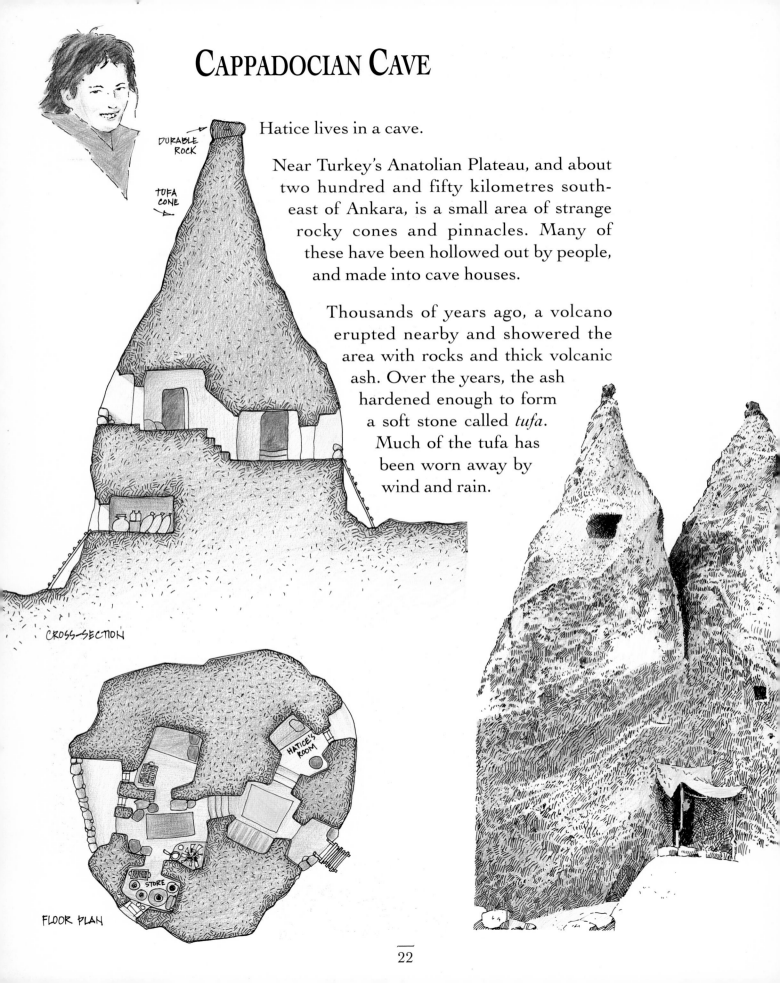

DURABLE ROCK

TUFA CONE

Hatice lives in a cave.

Near Turkey's Anatolian Plateau, and about two hundred and fifty kilometres south-east of Ankara, is a small area of strange rocky cones and pinnacles. Many of these have been hollowed out by people, and made into cave houses.

Thousands of years ago, a volcano erupted nearby and showered the area with rocks and thick volcanic ash. Over the years, the ash hardened enough to form a soft stone called *tufa*. Much of the tufa has been worn away by wind and rain.

CROSS-SECTION

HATICE'S ROOM

STORE

FLOOR PLAN

But where large hard rocks had fallen, the tufa immediately underneath them did not get eroded.

The small region of Cappadocia where Hatice lives was first established as a religious retreat by the early Christians. At one time, 30,000 people lived here. Today, most of the caves are derelict. Some are used for storage by the local farmers, some are open to tourists, and a few are still occupied as houses. Very occasionally, a new one is hollowed out.

Hatice's cone house is ideally suited to the climate. It remains cool and dark on the hottest of days. Inside, the walls are painted white and hung with locally woven rugs. On the floor are more rugs and many brightly coloured cushions. In the main room there is a fireplace for cooking, and producing heat in winter.

NEW MEXICAN PUEBLO

Crucita lives in a *pueblo,* or village, in New Mexico.

The pueblos were originally built by Zuni and Tewa peoples, and later occupied by Navajo and Apaches. The pueblos are now centres of culture for many different native Americans.

CROSS-SECTION

A pueblo is like a block of flats with many homes in one building. Originally, there were no doors or windows on the ground floor, and the only way in was by ladder to the upper levels. Some pueblos are built of stone, but most are adobe, which is mud or clay bricks dried in the sun and then built into walls which are plastered over with more wet mud. The adobe walls are thick and stocky with only small openings for doors and windows. The roofs, which slope slightly to allow the rain to run off, are supported on logs called *vigas*. Trees are scarce in New Mexico, so the vigas may be used over and over again as old houses fall down and new ones are built. The ends of the vigas are never cut off—the extra length may be needed next time—and so they always stick out from the walls. There are some vigas in Crucita's village which are over nine hundred years old.

The people who live here practise many traditional arts and crafts. They have chosen to retain much of their traditional way of life and refused to have electricity and running water connected to the village.

The curious houses pictured above are in the village of Belas, in Syria.
They are built entirely of mud, but their shape is remarkably similar to
both the grass houses shown on page 18 and the stone houses on
pages 37.

Below, another densely packed village in Morocco.

4
HOUSES OF WOOD

NORTHERN EUROPE, RUSSIA and North America were, until only a hundred years ago, almost completely covered by huge, unbroken areas of forest. Timber was the obvious choice of building material for people living among mighty trees supplying an abundance of tall, straight, easily worked softwood.

Wood is light and strong and can span great distances. It can be cut and shaped for many purposes, or it can be used just as it is, to make the thick strong walls of a log cabin.

The log house pictured above is from Kizhi in northern Russia. Everything in the house, from the walls and floors to the roof covering and even the gutters, is cut from the pine trees shown in the background.

AUSTRALIAN QUEENSLANDER

Bruce lives in a *Queenslander* in north-eastern Australia.

From the early days of European settlement in this area, a distinctive style of timber house evolved to meet the many challenges of a different country.

The Queenslander's main feature is that it is built about two metres above ground on a series of heavy wooden poles. This has a number of advantages. It allows air to circulate and cool the underneath of the house. It helps to stop the destructive local termites from eating the floor. It helps to keep the dangerous local snakes out of the house. It provides a useful area under the house where clothes can dry during the wet season and a sheltered place where children can play and where odd jobs and outdoor work can be done.

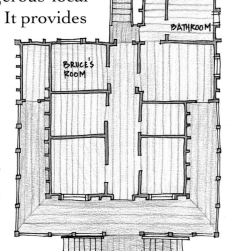

FLOOR PLAN

SIDE ELEVATION

Many of the early Queenslanders were built by pioneering farming families, like Bruce's grandparents, from the limited range of milled timber then available. At first they were light and flimsy buildings providing little protection against the heat. Verandahs were soon added to shade the walls of the house, and they became important rooms in their own right.

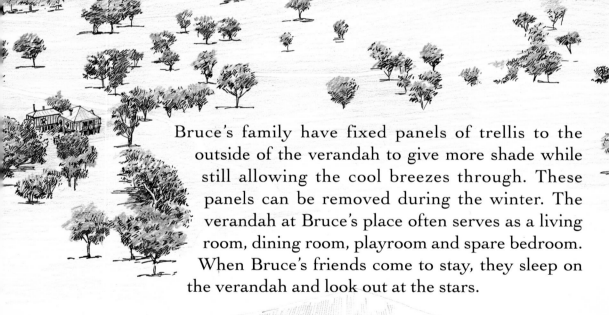

Bruce's family have fixed panels of trellis to the outside of the verandah to give more shade while still allowing the cool breezes through. These panels can be removed during the winter. The verandah at Bruce's place often serves as a living room, dining room, playroom and spare bedroom. When Bruce's friends come to stay, they sleep on the verandah and look out at the stars.

FRONT ELEVATION

JAPANESE MINKA

Naoko and Hiroshi live in a Japanese *minka,* or farmhouse.

Each part of Japan has its own particular style of minka, depending on the local materials available and on the climate. In Naoko and Hiroshi's area it is extremely cold so the minka is built to house the family, together with many farm activities, the stables, and storerooms, all under one huge, thatched roof. The house is also strong enough to carry the weight of winter snow.

The minka is built around a framework of thick wooden posts, roughly made out of tree trunks and branches. Each post stands on a large, round rock. The walls are made of bamboo woven together and then plastered with mud. The massive thatched roof is made of dried grass and supported on a timber and bamboo framework. Nails and screws were not used in the traditional minkas.

CEILING SPACE IS USED FOR SILKWORM CULTIVATION

CROSS-SECTION

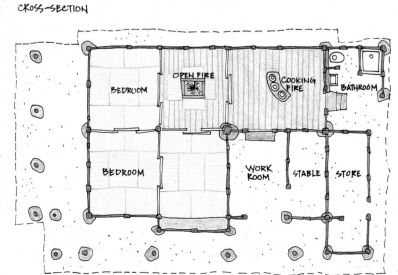

BEDROOM
OPEN FIRE
COOKING FIRE
BATHROOM
BEDROOM
WORK ROOM
STABLE
STORE

FLOOR PLAN

Instead, the framing pieces were carefully notched together or lashed with rope.

In the past, all the farmers in a small area would help each other with their farm work and with the jobs of building and repairing the minkas. The minkas were grouped together for protection, and so that the farmers could help each other.

These isolated farming communities used to grow or make everything they needed in the village. Today, the farmers have cars and tractors. There are modern roads, and Naoko and Hiroshi go to school in the nearby town where their family can shop for their daily needs.

But they still live in their comfortable, old minka.

Wooden houses, old and new: the timber framed house shown above was built nearly one thousand years ago. It is a farmhouse in Essex, England. The house on the right is in Auckland, New Zealand. Many grand wooden houses like this were built last century in the United States and the British colonies.

5 HOUSES OF STONE

STONE IS THE most highly valued of all building materials. Throughout history, different communities have reserved it for their most important buildings. We still do. This is because good building stone is strong, hard and durable. But it is usually difficult to obtain and difficult to work. Some areas, however, are lucky to have plenty of relatively soft stone. In these places, people build stone houses.

Cotswold Cottage

Albert lives in a Cotswold cottage.

The Cotswold is a region in the west of England famed for its attractive stone cottages and little villages. For many hundreds of years, stonemasons have built houses here from the local *eggstone* or *oolite* (a kind of limestone).

The walls are painstakingly put together without mortar, almost like a jigsaw puzzle. Even the roof is made of slabs of the same stone pegged onto a timber frame with oak pegs. The roofing slabs come in almost thirty different sizes, each with its own peculiar name, like Long Bachelors and Short Wivetts. The biggest slabs (over one metre long) are laid at the bottom of the roof slope, and the smallest at the top. The roofs are steeply pitched to allow the heavy rain and snow to run off easily.

The windows in these houses are usually small, not because of the climate but because glass was a rare and expensive material when most of them were built.

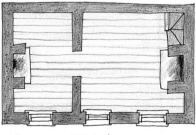

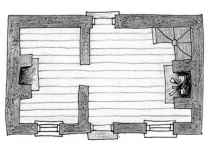

ROOF SHOWING BATTENS

WALL

CROSS-SECTION

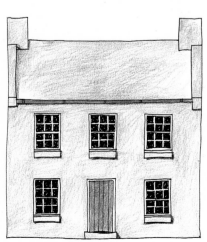

FRONT ELEVATION

UPPER FLOOR PLAN

GROUND FLOOR PLAN

APULIAN TRULLO

Aldo lives in a *trullo* in a small village in southern Italy.

Three hundred years ago, the local baron, Gian Girolamo II, the 'one-eyed', hit on a way of reducing the amount of taxes he had to pay to the king. The tax was, at that time, based on the number of houses in his domain.

Gian Girolamo II ordered his subjects to build their stone houses without mortar so that they could be dismantled easily should the king's tax inspector pay a visit.

This scheme, together with the large number of limestone rocks lying around waiting to be used, led to the distinctive shape of the trullo. Trulli were originally built with stones gathered up from the fields. There were so many stones lying around that, even when all the buildings, fences and roads were built entirely of stone, there were still so many left that they had to be piled up in corners of the paddocks to get them out of the way.

LOOKING UP INTO THE DOME. EACH RING OF STONES IS A LITTLE SMALLER THAN THE ONE BELOW.

DOMES ARE MADE OUT OF TWO SKINS OF STONE

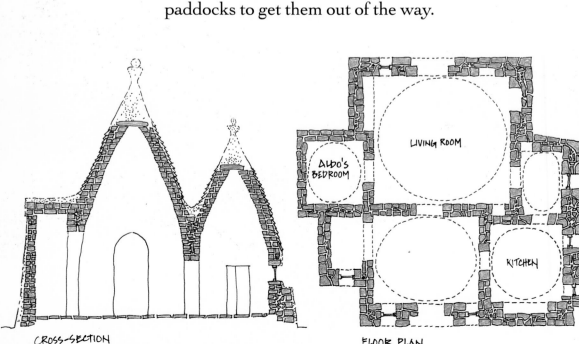

CROSS-SECTION

FLOOR PLAN

ALDO'S BEDROOM

LIVING ROOM

KITCHEN

Each trullo consists of a series of square rooms with conical roofs. The walls and roofs are built of two skins of stone, and the cavity in between is filled with rubble. The cones are made of successive rings of stone blocks. Each ring is a little smaller than the one below. The walls and the very top of the cones are covered with dazzling white lime-plaster, and the cones have an extra layer of flat stones to keep them dry. This seems like a rather unstable and dangerous method of building a roof, but it works as long as the rooms are not too big. Indeed, the largest room ever successfully roofed in this way is only six metres square.

Water collected from the roofs is channelled into underground tanks cut out of the rock.

Aldo and his family do much of their living, cooking, eating and household tasks outdoors. The trulli are very dark and cool in the hot Mediterranean summer, but they can be cold, damp and uncomfortable in wintertime.

The weight of the thick, heavy slates has warped and buckled the roof of this old stone farmhouse in Cornwall. The small room on the near corner is a recent addition.

Below, a small stone farmhouse and barn in County Galway, Ireland. The thatched roof is tied down with diagonal strands of rope.

GLOSSARY

ADOBE — Wall construction method using sun-dried mud bricks finished with wet mud.

ARCH — Curved structure over a door or window supporting the upper part of a building.

BATTENS — Thin pieces of wood fixed to the roof frame to support the roofing material.

CONE — An object with a wide circular base, a smaller circular top and sloping sides.

CORRUGATED IRON — Manufactured steel roofing material.

DOME — Roof in the shape of half a hollow ball.

ELEVATION — Side view of a building drawn to scale.

GABLE — Vertical, triangular end of a ridged roof.

GRANARY — Store for keeping grain (e.g. wheat, rice).

HEARTH — Stone, brick or concrete base of a fireplace or cooking fire.

LATTICE — see *trellis*.

LIME-PLASTER — Mixture of lime, sand and water which is spread onto a wall; when dry it forms a hard smooth surface.

MORTAR — Mixture of sand, cement, lime and water used to bind brick or stone walls together.

PITCH — Slope (of a roof).

REED — Tall, thick and strong kind of grass used in buildings, thatching, floor mats, and some structural framing.

SLATES — Thin stone roofing material.

SOFTWOOD — Timber from pine and some similar trees (all wood is classified as either softwood or hardwood).

SPIRAL — Coil created by curving continuously around a fixed point while moving steadily away from it.

STABLE — Building where horses live.

STONEMASON — Tradesperson who works with stone.

TIMBER — Wood which has been cut and milled.

TRELLIS — Grating of thin pieces of wood or metal.

THATCH — Roofing material made of grass.

INDEX